Kissing In The Kitchen
*verses of challenged love
& recipes for relief*

By

Betsy Ratner

© Copyright 2000 by Betsy Ratner

All rights reserved.
Published in the United States by:
Ⓜ Metacognitive Press
P.O. Box 5042
Woodbridge, CT 06525

Library of Congress Control Number: 00-092822
Ratner, Betsy
Kissing in the Kitchen
ISBN 0-9704622-0-4

Dedication

*This book is dedicated to my sister Cindy,
who is battling Huntington's Disease
&
In loving memory of my sisters,
Nancy and Nora,
and my father, Harold.*

Acknowledgements

My husband Artie's love, support, and encouragement
Our terrific son
My parents' undying love
My sisters' sharing
Mom's continuous strength to cope
Abraham's ongoing spiritual guidance
The inspiration from the
          Woodbridge Women's Writer's Group

Special Thanks

Michael Iannuzzi & Tyco Copy Center
- Susan Goolsby
- Brendee Mendlesohn
- Denise Shaw
- Donna Levine
- Tom Strong
- Debbie Pucillo
- Linda Scranton
- Pamela Begin
- Penny Merriam
- Louise Waugh
- Gloria Duhl
- Macaire Stein
- Woodbridge Town Library Reference Librarians
- Edward J. McCarthy
- Rick Kaletsky
- Harry Rosenberg
- Helen Rosenberg

Preface

Through writing, my heart gave way to the pen and the words lifted the pain. The release of feelings was cathartic. The emergence of a smile upon my face peered through the darkness as the ink washed over the paper erasing the discomforts. The recipes for my relief are marked upon the pages of **Kissing in the Kitchen**.

This book has allowed me to tell my heartfelt story. It may offer others an opportunity to see the discovery of truth and light through love. My family and I experienced huge difficulties watching our loved ones (sisters and father's) deterioration due to Huntington's Disease (a motor neuron degenerative illness). My family's journey is so remarkable. It is filled with devastation and loving-kindness. I believe sharing my reflections, not only provides an outlet, but leaves a legacy. Through the words, I feel, as you possibly will, satisfaction, strength and comfort.

Life's personal challenges are many. Through poetic interludes that entwine the hardships and turn them amazingly into joys, **Kissing in the Kitchen** (as my parents often did) will offer you the chance to melt away your fears, worries and anxieties. Each poem provokes a story for you to relate to personally. The words regale many life changes in numerous ways. Hopefully, you will be totally entranced into a new way to view life's experiences. The once huge mountains will become dunes of sand which are blown away in the wind,

Preface continued...

leaving only their beauty and goodness behind.
 I believe the different experience of looking beyond and seeing things in unusual ways, will truly excite you into realizing that life can become more lovingly joyful and that you have the power to bring it forth. I hope inspiration takes hold and you discover that your wishes and dreams can prevail.

Introduction
Miles of Amazing Resilience

"How many miles do you have on them?," she asked as she pointed to Mom's clasped hands, watching her thumbs continually twirl around each other in a fast-paced, seemingly endless motion. Hysterical laughter broke out for all Mom was doing was her usual, harmless, contemplative daydreaming. Mother had married a marvelous man with whom she shared love and a world filled with magnificent pleasures; from five beautiful daughters to an exquisitely huge home filled with an abundance of joy, health, and love! Art lessons, baking, travel, cooking, swimming, skating and carpooling her children filled her glorious days.

Who could have known? The diabolical was yet to occur. Slowly, ever so slowly, strange unknown behaviors that never matched her mate before crept into their daily lives. Oh, the torment and pain that was experienced by all. Mom anguished over her dear husband's neurological and muscular disorder. He could not control any of his movements. Some dementia was also sneaking in. As Huntington's disease attacked her true love, their days were changed forever.

Thumb-mile pondering continued. Mom gained strength through her daily support of her darling love by fulfilling each of his needs. Out went the scrumptious luncheons with friends, the vigorous tennis and golf games, as well as the magnificent museum escapades. In its place was an undying devotion to the daily care of her love.

Introduction continued...

As the thumbs kept going round and round, balance and resilience prevailed. More than basic existence was needed to survive this trauma. The love of her family and the strength of her spirit brought her salvation and sustenance.

Accomplishments

"There are doers and dreamers", Dad expounded as we rode in his precious '65 white Continental. Living in the moment and letting that moment consistently carry you on to life's next wonderful place is how Dad lived. As a risk taker, there was no obstacle he would not overcome or any challenge he felt too difficult.

Dad was a true entrepreneur. He learned to scuba dive in order to retrieve a supposedly unsalvageable '43 foot ketch. Dad restored a junked 1908 Franklin, in which he drove us to the Woodbridge Orchards for his sumptuous cider and delectable fresh apples. His display of remarkable business acumen was evidenced by his balancing of his automobile dealership with his real estate ventures. Gifted verbal skills would help this self-made giant attain whatever he needed in order to catch his dreams.

Dad's creativity, keen insight, and uncanny intuition, coupled with his natural practical knowledge and synthesizing abilities aided him in grasping all that he wanted. His passion, was bringing the finest of everything to his loved ones.

Introduction continued...

However, he was able to instill in his five daughters the importance of hard work. He stated in order to live each day to its fullest and attain your goals, we needed to dedicate ourselves to use our time wisely, commit ourselves to stay on task and work hard for what we wanted. This would help us to catch the brass ring of life's carousel.

Dad's great love was modeled again and again as I spied Mom and him kissing in the kitchen. This display of affection, along with all the special daily things Dad did for Mom and all five children, helped model incredible love. This great love is mirrored in each of his offspring's marriages. We are so fortunate to have this gift; the ability to manifest the intangible: love.

Strong love continued through all the stages of Huntington's disease. Even when he coughed, often choking, he would say after catching his breath, that it was all right. It was only his disease. Don't worry. After fighting and struggling with the disease for years, Dad learned to face this challenge differently. He decided to make peace with it and to be as graceful as possible through the last stages. His eyes always showed this with the love that poured from them when he could not speak any more. Dad would watch you circle around his bed, waiting for you to land another big kiss on his cheek.

Each of his daughters remember the fun of Dad shooting hoops in the driveway, chopping and carrying wood for the fireplace, toasting

Introduction continued…

marshmallows and making popcorn. We recall being on Dad's lap learning to drive the tractor to mow the lawn. Also, Dad running along side of the first two wheelers brings smiles to our faces. Dad was full of encouraging words as he pushed us along the road. We realized Dad truly taught us to pedal down our own challenging highways and discover the world.

There are doers and dreamers, Dad was both.

Table of Contents

I. Eruption and Challenges
  Necessity 2
  See it! Taste it! Touch it! 3
  The Smell in the Elevator 4
  An Old Train Ride 5
  Pumping Pain 6
  Eruption of Life 7
  Enhanced Resistance 8
  Enlightened 9
  Ready 10
  Terrific Torment 11
  Engine Room 12
  A Forced Peace 13
  Gone Fishing 14
  Reality 15
  Living With Disease 15
  Rolling Life 15
  Challenges 15

II. Love
  The Magical Dance 17
  The Son Continues to Shine 19
  Reverence 20
  Dad's Strength 21
  Cindy's Own Way 22
  Red Flowering Grace 24
  Dad's Love 27
  A Smile to the Land .28
  Loving Surprise 29
  Remarkable Blonde .30
  Dependent 31

Table of Contents continued...

Love continued...
    Authentic Power 32
    Bonus 33
    Snuggle 34
    Harmonious Beauty 34
    Love 34
    Fearful Love 35
    Spontaneous Gorgeous Greeting 36
    Greatness 37
    Harvesting Happiness 38
    The Continuum 39
    Hide and Seek 40
    Passion of the Soul 41
    Glad to Find G-d 43

III. Hope and Wonders
    Cultivate and Cherish 45
    Peace 46
    Of the Days 46
    Understory 46
    Where? 47
    Always 47
    Strength 47
    The Music Played On 48
    Growth 48
    Frolic 48
    Riding On 49
    Coping 49
    Finding Rest 49
    Contentment 50
    Reaching 50
    Gentle Light 50
    We Do it All 51

Table of Contents continued...
Ah! Ah! 52
Captured in a Car 53

Hopes and Wonders continued...
   Time 54
   Open 54
   Energy 54
   Going On 54
   Pairs of Thankfulness 55
   Loss and Gain 57
   Successful Inspiration 58

Conclusion 59

Eruption and Challenges

Necessity

A story that needs to be told
By the very brave and bold.
A family of seven,
Three presently in heaven.
All had to learn
How to cope
Being in the same boat.
HD had stricken
Time was a tickin'.

See it! Taste it! Touch it!

Inspired, excited, filled with hope
Knowing and assured to cope.
With time and work
Trust and care do lurk.
Behind each idea
A promised panacea.
Elation filled path
Success making splash.
Can taste the look
Of a great book!

The Smell In The Elevator

Down to the basement
To the unknown fear.
Letting go inside.
Scared, bewildered,
Unsure and apprehensive.
Alone,
Nothing to do.
No friends, no busy activities.
Will it ever change?
When can it be different?
Look at life out the window.
Passersby are laughing and going places.
Life seems so natural and normal for them.
I want it to be like that.
Will it be?
Can smiles come again?

An Old Train Ride

Chugging along, back in time
Listening to the whistle stop
And the horn blowing.
As the diesel engine pulls us forward,
Looking above the windows,
The paint crackled like the spider's home.
Between the lines.
The hovered sound screeched.
Talking about the good days,
With the fun, frolic and love making joys
To the creative, explorative decisions.
The fingers of the web,
Each having a memory
Before the shock took hold.
And then it stopped!

Pumping Pain

Pain, missing who they were,
Where did they go?
How did it happen?
Why on earth?
A nightmare!
Cannot find the answers.
There is no reason.
Life goes on.
Finding ways to move ahead.
Gaze into the water.
Walk along the stream.
Wade in the ocean,
Or simply, dream.
What really works
Is up to you.
Make a conscious effort
To do what you must do.
Generate some wishes.
Move amongst the stars.
Remember who you are,
Peace is at your grasp.
Love is always central.
It is, but the task
To go beyond the fury
With the clover and the curry.
Whether it is cuisine,
Sporting, or sculpting
That keeps you keen,
Go with the flow
Onward with your path
Because the well,
Deserve the aftermath!

Eruption of Life

Uncomfortably jagged
Scary, fear revisited,
Untamed mind,
Why?
What is going on?
What is coming?
Control!
How?
Pray, relax, meditate,
Breathe, focus
Positive thoughts.
Have confidence,
Surrender the soul
To reverence
And soaring spirits.
To the joys of life
Bringing soothing,
Cherished healings,
To conceal the scars
On the continuous journey.
To unfold
The dark
And bring the light.
To refresh, renew,
Revitalize life.
And build a new landscape
For deserved pleasures!

Enhanced Resistance

Anxious, uneasy and unsure,
Helpless and afraid,
Strange, weird and different
Bizarre behavior
Diabolical personality
Unusual response
Not the norm!
Burdens galore,
Difficult to help.
Stay, leave or go?
Together, separate
On, off
Bewildered movement
Enhanced resistance.

Enlightened

Reconnoiter, regroup, reencounter
Renew, refresh, refinish.
Step back then forward,
As the recipe changes
Add a spoonful of love.
Simmer a while,
Now a pinch of prayer
In order to manage.
Move to start again,
Make a new plan
Knowing that you can.
Rekindle, reconnect, reenter
The place before you fell.

Ready

Free, alive, exciting.
Joyous, ready, and willing.
Capable, energetic
And open, accepting what is.
Able to take the challenge.
Honest, motivated, and hard working.
Can do the tasks
For what it takes.
Want the process.
Accepting results.

Terrific Torment

Missed the bed,
Stumbled into the chair
Tripped over her feet
Disastrous triumph
No breaks.
Helmet secure,
Gait unsteady
Rambling voice
Flailing arms
Fidgety twisted head
Utensils missing mouth.
Digits flying about
Constant movement
Unknowing confusion.
Boyfriend nearby
Blind and talkative.
Definite caring and security
Together happy and sharing
Smiling true fun love.

Engine Room

It smelled like oil
With the generator going.
Knobs, levers,
Pulleys and buttons there
To grab.
If it is all too much,
The handle was there
To pull you forward
Or tug you back.
Choices you must make,
To help you move on
Or just to fasten you down.
To charge you ahead
Majestically with vigor
And to defeat the surge.
Will you spring forward and go?
Or will it hold you in tow?

A Forced Peace

Thumb turns,
To stomach churns.
The torment
And the pain.
Hurt clear through.
Anguish inside,
Trying to find
Ways to change
The incredible madness.
Begin to look at it
In a different way
And befriend the agony.
Sit with it,
Because
It has become my company.

Gone Fishing

I gave a wet noodle yawn,
Because I was exhausted and limp.
Completely spent
And truly all gone,
I was drained of energy.
Very tired and weary
With a dwindling mind,
My dawdling legs
Coupled by my downward head
Had me moving with a dangly limp,
Drooping and moping
With drizzling tears
Falling backward onto the bed.
Dripping like an ice cream cone
On a hot sidewalk.
Hoping, rest and sleep
Would bring a recharge.
A return to "al dente."

Reality

Morning patches
Anxiety unveiled
Revealing the world.

Living With Disease

Black forest run
Breathtaking back water
Rushing against the wind.

Rolling Life

Metamorphic greens
Churning time forever
Leaving love in tow.

Challenges

Bouquet of butterflies
Strange pincushion
Marbleized life.

Love

The Magical Dance

Happiness sprang
Tears of joy.
Goose bumps galore
And chills along my spine.
As he chanted
With poise
And dignity
Grace and presence
We were so proud to recall
From whence he came,
To see where he's been
And know where he is going.
What a great successful journey!

Copacetic son shines
Maturity, growing
Learning life's lessons
With confidence.
Becoming strong and willing
Ready and independent.
Going on with sturdy stature
Moving forward with vigor
And pride
As well as joy.
Aiming high,

Learning and wanting more
Showing a glow
To succeed with a symbiotic happiness.

The Magical Dance continued…

Prayers answered
That's our boy
He's back
Joy, excitement,
And enthusiasm radiating
From each and every pore.
Spilling smiles with happy glows,
Enthralled with inner pride.

Expressing true leadership
Bringing fulfillment.
Carrying abundance
Of perseverance and success
From the honored commitment
And motivation.
We are so proud!

The Son Continues to Shine

He is so special
And truly appreciated
Understood and aiming high.
Reaching beyond
Happy to be on the righteous journey.
The hard work
Paves the way to success.
Hours of toil
Pounding onward
Forgetting the past and
Reaching anew.

Reverence

Bittersweet dreams
Fill the shuddered room.
There is a shaking
Yet a solace.
Some peace emerges with
Love amongst the racking movements
And torrents of restfulness.
There they lie,
Mother and child.
Relief…
All right to go on,
Well to continue.
Glad to go on
Refreshed, revitalized
Renewed, ready
Happy and content.
With smiles and joy,
Back to normal.
Time to work.
Time to play.
Enjoy the world again!

Dad's Strength

Loving and caring
Enveloped his children,
Devoted to his family,
Protecting and educating,
Exposing culture.
Prompting new experiences,
Expounding,
"Travel brings knowledge!"
"Books help you grow!"
Encouraging reading,
The Wall Street Journal,
His Bible that helped
With his keen business
Insights that seeded ideas.
Supporting those in need,
And all important causes.
Sensitivity and awareness
To bring out the best
Of those in his nest.
Of love and devotion,
Dad built confidence
To help us understand
We can do anything
And make a difference.
As he did!

Cindy's Own Way

Shinning, twinkling eyes
Smiling from ear to ear
Joy and happiness
Emanating.
Energy abound
With laughter galore,
Whole body giggles coupled by
Infectious hysterics.
The contagious thrill
Overflows her heart with love.
Optimistic and encouraging
As well as hopeful and accepting
She's an inspiration to us all.
As she resides in a hall
Filled with patients with pasts.
Brilliant business woman
Always successful.
Constantly making deals
Had the midas touch.
Enjoyed challenges
Donning stunning outfits
With gorgeous taste,
The beautiful brunette,
Gloriously animated
Loved to chat.
Like Dad wanted only the best.
Explored new endeavors,
Like real estate investments
And gold mine ventures.

Cindy's Own Way continued…

Although the childhood memories,
Clear as a bell
Of ice skating at Greely's Rink
And being a camper and counselor
Lead us to recalling her
Happy adventures at Laurelwood.
Only the love can guide us through,
The difficult road
She will wheel and move.
As she pedals the mini red Austin
Down the driveway of life,
It is now,
Into the unknown strife.

Red Flowering Grace

Nancy was more poetic than a story
Truly a morning glory.
She lit up the world with her smile
As she often walked many a mile.
Togetherness brought her treasures
As nature's wonders gave her pleasures.
For she loved the fauna and flora
As did our dear Nora.
Disease dealt a poor favor
Family visits were her savior.
But despite, there was peace
For she declared a new lease.
To accept her fate
With incredible grace,
Although it was rough
She was remarkably tough.
Inspired by all
However...she did fall.
After breaking her hip
She took quite a dip.
If we look back
Despite the lack
Of Nancy's sound
And joy abound.
We Remember…
Sharing a bedroom and selecting violet colors for
    the walls.
Walking to the Woodbridge Country Club to swim.
Sledding and arguing whose turn it was to drag the
    toboggan back up hill.

Red Flowering Grace continued…

Performing plays for our parents and neighbors,
Creating dances and songs together.
Eating candy and getting cavities.
Walking, no racing to the school bus stop.
Being on the same tribe at Camp Laurelwood.
Snacking en route to Hebrew school.
Disputing whose turn for dishwashing.
Dividing the line for raking the lawn and then
       piling the leaves and jumping in covering
       each other to scare another sibling.
The two of us playing the guitar, one rock and the
       other classical.
Using the family clothes to dress our snow families
Creating igloos after a snowball fight and testing
       how warm it was inside.
Building forts to hold snack parties with friends
Making mud pies in the backyard.
Helping Dad with the 1908 Franklin,
And riding in it with the family to the
       apple orchard.
Eating a pumpkin pie solo!
Cindy and Nancy fighting about nothing, "Mom,
       she hit me!" Then shaking hands and
       kissing and all was well again.
She wore my sweater and stretched it, or I wore
       it and got it dirty.
Sister meetings at the night light to chat while
       roasting marshmallows.
Nancy displayed an artistic nature wearing vintage
       clothing as she is now.

Red Flowering Grace continued…

She adored children.
She loved to teach.
Enjoyed social occasions,
And had incredible humor.

Nancy, our natural beauty
Turned heads when she went by.
She portrayed:
> Exquisite features
> Gorgeous, magnificent locks
> Elegant, quiet radiance
> A convivial smile
> Abundant, artful passion
> Sublime friendship
> And courageous embodied love!

    Her hugs lasted forever. You'd be numb before long, but she never wanted to release you. I can still feel her arms around me.
    We will remember her mindful spirit and heartful soul, because Nancy's beauty and presence spoke volumes.
    The delicacy of her stoic, heroic, strength, grace and pulchritude will endure. Nancy, our delicate rose, we will love you always!

Dad's Love

The complexities of Dad,
Figuring out where he was
With the hidden personality masked by the disease.

Only time and love
As well as spirit and emotion
Showed us the difference
And bought some peace and solace.

We will always treasure the teachings,
The kindnesses, the caring and understanding,
The believing, the striving and the attaining!

For as Dad's soul is with us,
He continues to guide us through life's intricacies,
Showing us the righteous paths,
Through his bond of love!

A Smile to the Land

She's always there,
Our angel Nora.
Her uplifting love
Puts a smile on my face.
With her guidance and support
I feel compelled to create.
Each step of the way,
She is taking my hand
Across the land
Filling me with happiness and success.

Loving Surprise

Unlimited planning
With true sharing
Empathetic caring
And incredible organization,
Creative invitations
Numerous secret phone calls
Scrumptious delicious foods,
Many friends
Hidden time and space
Numerous shopping sprees.
Delightful hospitality
With clever camouflaging.
Loaded with unique ideas
And extravagant favors
For meaningful honors,
Milestone celebrations.
Surprise… fun…
Love!

Remarkable Blonde

The other well one,
With remarkable intelligence.
Ebullient personality
Sparkling and shining with glee.
Full of humor and wit
Enormous, serious laughter.
Extremely, engaging giggles
Continuous, contagious fun,
Exhausting, timeless energy
Helps us all feel better.

Dependent

Unsure when
Change will occur.
When he will grow up
See the light.
That the weekend poison
Keeps him tight.
So growth is slow.
To go beyond
It is up to him.
To take a stand,
To make a move
Out of the groove.
To reach out
Go beyond,
Find the strength
To understand.
He can make it
The power is there.
He knows where
From within he stares.
Watching is tough.
Finding a way is rough.
It is his ownership
His path to follow
So I will not wallow.

Authentic Power

Again he touched someone
And changed their lives.
He made them better than before.
Generous and gentle
As well as kind and caring.
He is full of compassion
And loaded with empathy.
These are the traits
Of a son and a true friend.
When shared by another,
The recipient of the gifts;
How outstandingly supportive and special.
Our offspring has been and still is.
Pride wells up to the wet eyes
Tears envelop the joys.
For we always knew the treasures he held
And quietly shared in private.
The written recognition from others,
And the participation of the retelling
Brings it back home again with
Droplets of enchanted pleasures,
Of harmonic peace!
The world is a better place
Because of him!

Bonus

Happiness glowing
From my heart,
With tears of joy
Flowing down my cheeks.
As I recall the words sung by him,
Sharing his pride of doing so well
With his new endeavor.
Pounding, throbbing,
Racing with ravenous rapture
For the thrill,
Excitement and bounty,
G-d has brought
To all of us!

Snuggle

Spooning with frenzy,
Creating a trance of intoxication.
Inspired by the feast,
That relished each touch.
Reaching exaltation,
Transporting to paradise

Harmonious Beauty

Bodies on the candied pillows,
Singing blankets cover us.
Dreams melting troubles to pudding,
Exploding love spilling upon the sheets.

Love

Soul infusement occurs,
With the dance.
As all else is abandoned,
I find myself wrapped in delightful passion!

Fearful Love

Together,
Dancing in joy.
Each dining and pleasing
With delectable treats.
Hand in hand,
Arm in arm,
Sitting on laps,
Rubbing his back.
Hugs upon hugs,
Kissing full of tongue.
Touching and caressing,
While pressing.
Loving pleasures,
Ecstatic delight,
Holding on tight,
With great might.
Never wanting to let go,
Afraid it is so,
That with weight in tow,
It will take him slow.

Spontaneous Gorgeous Greeting

Door opens,
Feel the flow.
Smiles hold fast.
Enter together
Embracing beauty
Bringing wonderful bonds of
Hugs, pulls, and tugs of passion
Coupled by grabbing grasps of moist kisses
And squeezes with teases.
Hearts moving as one
Hot, fuzzy tastes
Of scented yummy stickiness
And dancing sounds
Pursuing the passionate stars,
Forming superb, magnificent pleasures
Skyrocketing, breathtaking heights
As splendid love continues!

Greatness

G-d, prayer, strength and smile
All part of the amplitudinal mile.
Abundance and might transcend,
Bringing faith to lend.
Continue to reach for more.
It is behind every door.
The magnitude of distinction
Is stupendous in its reason.
To follow your heart
Put the horse ahead of the cart.
Move forward with your idea.
It can be a panacea,
For you and others to follow.
So as not to wallow
As you create, invent and find anew,
As each of us should do!

Harvesting Happiness

Enter hardy laughter
With embracing personal fun
And pervading humor beyond.
Along with glorious giggles galore
We have quiet, hysterical pain,
Huge smiles
And tears abound,
Coupled with contagious, loving laughs,
And cries beaming gleefully.
Making the endorphins flow
With cascading good feelings.
Entwined with blissful exhaustion
As well as heightened joy.
Leaving ecstasy to prevail!

The Continuum

Friendships ebb and flow,
Time passes.
Work to be done,
Building relationships.
Through listening, trusting,
Sharing and caring.
Not always with ease,
Tenuously holding on
To goodness and truth
With spiritful help
Which lessens the load.
With great support
Moving the obstructions,
And shedding the weights
Finds that the release brings
A new freshness to go on.

Hide and Seek

Excruciating as it is
And wanting to run and hide,
Reconnoiter and plow through.
Love and joy is there.
Excitement and pleasures
Are yours for the taking.
Finding your release,
Write, draw, sing, dance or meditate
Alone, or with a mate.
Love will provide.
Grab a hug and another look.
Relax and read this book,
Because all it takes is you,
Learning to look at things anew.
Put the anxiety and confusion,
As well as the trembling
And bewilderment behind you.
Happiness exists within each of us!

Passion of the Soul

Feel the whirl
And twirl.
Moving free
About the room.
Flying across spaces
Like a bird
On a delightful journey.
Feet sliding on the floor
Like ice.
Open and carefree
As an air blown leaf.
A unique form
Portrayed in the vast spaces.
Slippery actions giving way to
Opportunity and fortune.
Completely available knowing
Nothing is impossible.
No holds barred
True happiness expressed
With each sway of the body.
Unusual angular
Unlimited smiling signs
Of joy shown on a beaming shadow,
Making curling ribbon paths.
Heavenly probing
Explorations continue,
Displaying unbelievable fun
Beyond the surface
Bringing excitement
With pure pleasure.

Passion of the Soul continued…

While absorbing the patterned vibrations,
And the beating and tapping rhythms,
Feel the cool air against the sweet sweat,
As sailing continues across the sky.
Spinning diversely
Round and round
Seeing blurred colors
Curving about
Throngs of people mesmerized,
Transfixed on each and every movement
As I drink in the euphoria!

Glad To Find G-d

Happy, joyful, full of glee,
Delighted, cheerful, willing.
All beautiful, jubilant, carefree,
Raptured enjoyment, rejoicing
That G-d is esteemed and almighty.
Dignified, majestic alrighty,
His greatness transcends,
Bringing peace to the land.
If you find it within,
The power you will win!

*Hope
and
Wonders*

Cultivate and Cherish

The most exquisite blue
Below us in the grotto,
Looks heavenly
As though the sun peers through
The cracks in the caves.
It is so mesmerizing.
It is impossible to move on.
The group is nowhere in sight.
I am transfixed.
The wet, wonders
With the azure brilliance,
Reflects and reverberates.
It goes through to the soul.
What remarkable beauty.
I cannot budge.
I want to stay forever,
Simply staring at the awesomeness,
Drinking in the pleasure
In order to savor the treasure,
For future reflections of joy and peace
Bringing profound fulfilling nourishment.

Peace

Summer finally,
Smiling upon the grasses
Wandering toward the sky.

Of The Days

The taste of sunflowers
Showing memories
Light up my life.

Understory

Daisies come and daisies go
Carrying memories to and fro.
From the first kiss to wedded bliss
Whether treetops glow
Or the clouds flow.

Where?

Anxiously waited rain
Bleeding hearts
Finally came back home.

Always

Mother of dew
Belonging here
Rests upon the bed.

Strength

Touches of eagles
All part of us
Now and forever more.

The Music Played On

Birds chirping
Racing in my head
The sky is wide open.

Growth

Asters smiling
Upon the ceilings
Building new horizons

Frolic

Etched in stamen
Wonders hidden
Deer run with it all.

Coping

Silhouetted fall
Food shadows
Shoulder the magnificent fruits.

Riding On

Smooth cactus
Rush the field
With hope

Finding rest

A plethora of worry
Throw away cautions
Find harmony.

Contentment

Gumdrops on the hill
Snug shirts blanket the land
Forcing alluring fulfill ment.

Reaching

Triumphant avenues
Exceed expectations
Despite hardships.

Gentle Light

Delectable touch
Rests upon the lawn
Eating sweet kisses.

We Do it All

Women, strong, fortuitous,
Available to help
Despite the traumas.
Putting pieces together
Like a puzzle.
Bonding families
Making connections,
Holding strength to survive,
Leading the way
Aiding the cause
Binding with power.
Seeing and moving
Organizing and planning
Bringing success.
Showing and guiding
Giving peace and harmony.
Striving for growth and change,
Feel the ties
Giving grace and dignity.
Always there to facilitate
Behind the scenes
Giving closure
'Til the next time.
Women make the world flow!

Ah Ah

Luxury and delight,
With space spread out right
To relax, rest, read and write
Or visit, chat and watch the sights.
While enjoying the pleasures
Keeping in measure,
Treats galore
And service even more.
Hours passing
You are there
Totally without a care!

Captured in a Car

Two by two
On the move
Anything goes,
Forgetting tears and woes.
Anywhere, everywhere
Peace unfolding
Before your eyes.
Falls, peaks, valleys
And snow topped mountains
Along with sweet scented soil,
Orange to indigo sunsets
And teal skies
Of purple majesty.
Mesmerizing vistas
Endless flowing rivers
And gorgeous gorges,
Remarkable sites
Unpredictable beauty.
Luscious landscapes galore
True picturesque wonderment,
Of snowy patches
And hot, sunny, shimmering lakes
Capturing smiles of awe,
From warm, friendly faces.

Time

Steaming snow
Lethargic flowers
Pendulum continues to jump

Open

Shivering hair
Running free
As the clouds murmur.

Energy

Moss whispers
With an edible soul
The wind listens.

Going On

The breathing stones
Have a voice
Filled with precious love.

Pairs of Thankfulness

Preserved quiet and exciting noise
Powerful breathing and docile meditation.
Robust stretching and courageous growth
Embodied brilliance and emerging beauty.
Abundant love and artful passion
Caring people in ubiquitous places.
Comforting togetherness and supportive bonding
Ecstatic joy and cultivated happiness.
Original dance and unique music
Common strangeness and unusual familiarity.
Wonderful family and great friends
Fabulous health and extravagant wealth.
Unequaled time and undeniable space
Determined giving and some taking.
Infinite pride and absolute happiness
Strong comfort and true harmony.
Creative work and frivolous play
Productive reflections and glowing reports.
Fertile thinking and honest feelings
Fervent safety and vigilant security.
Lively body and generous soul
Invulnerable trust and unassailable care.
Various healings and diverse relaxations
Virtuous prayers and grand fulfillment.
Staunch frankness and invariable skepticism
Constant physical and unlimited spirituality.
Delicious textures and expansive tastes
Wafted scents and intuitive sense.
G-d's oneness and heaven's honor
Judicious sweetness and courageous tartness.

Pairs of Thankfulness continued…

Fruitful abundance and enlightened energy
Sharing pleasures and marvelous treasures.
Acute listening and sympathetic empathizing
Gloriously quiet and exciting moments.
Peaceful oceans and shimmering lakes
Wonderful fauna and lovely flora.
Incredible sounds and remarkable sights
One moment and endless time.
Mindful spirit and heartfelt soul
Breathing beings and the privilege of living.

Loss and Gain

Release words from your heart.
Let go of negative thoughts and feelings.
Make way for positive balance.
Problems can be all consuming.
Learn to respond to the sadness
By creating newness.
You are in the driver's seat
To decide to take control.
Adjust your attitude,
Choose to radiate love and compassion
In order to receive it in return.
Set the course for grace and beauty.
The world is yours.

Successful Inspiration

G-d has brought such love and delight
That the book came out just right.
It truly says what is needed,
To help build hope
For those to cope.

Conclusion

Although, we continue to deal with the loss of three immediate family members and have a loved one in a nursing home, we are fortunate that we have not perpetuated the illness. The disease ends for us, but we hope for a cure.

Please know that you are not alone. Use your spirit to help you find the joys, despite the hardships. Peace, coupled with love, is around the corner to guide you.

* (front cover) Proceeds (50 % of the profits) from **Kissing in the Kitchen** benefit Huntington's Disease Society of America's "Coalition for the Cure" and Grant and Fellowship Programs.

**To Purchase additional copies of Kissing in the Kitchen write:
Metacognitive Press (checks only)
P.O. Box 5042
Woodbridge, CT 06525
Send $11.95 + $3.50 shipping and handling/book**